Contents

Sensational Sculptures

I'm a **sculptor**. I make **sculptures** of groups of people by carving wood. Sculptures of people can be made of different materials.

These are made from rubbish like old cans and broken tiles. They might make us think about how much we throw away and how important recycling is.

These 6000 tiny **figures** are hand-painted. They are stuck on a wall in the shape of a map to make us think about where people live.

All over the world, you can see sensational sculptures of people. Let me show you some of my favourites!

The Terracotta Army

In 1974, some Chinese farmers were digging a well in a field. Suddenly, the spade hit something hard in the ground. At first, the farmers thought it was a big stone, but it wasn't. They had discovered a life-sized clay **warrior**.

More and more clay figures were uncovered. There were thousands of warriors hidden underground in large pits.

Over two thousand years ago, the First Emperor of China had ordered craftsmen to build the **terracotta** warriors. Maybe he thought they would protect him after he died.

The terracotta warriors may have been modelled on real people in the army. There are life-sized horses and chariots, too. It took more than 700 000 people nearly 40 years to build the army and their surroundings.

This warrior would have held a spear.

8

Workers dug clay from the earth to make the warriors. Craftsmen shaped the clay and let it dry. Then they baked it in a hot oven called a **kiln** to harden the clay.

The baked clay is called terracotta. Terracotta means 'baked earth'.

The sculptures have **solid** bases, but the upper bodies and heads are **hollow**. This helps them stand up. The craftsmen used **moulds** to make the legs, arms and heads.

They had about ten basic face-shape moulds that represented people from different areas of China.

Then they added details, like ears, beards and moustaches. Some warriors have plaited hair and others have their hair in a bun or wear hats.

Finally, they painted the warriors with paint and **lacquer**.

Nowadays, the warriors look grey, but they were brightly coloured when they were made.

Can you see the paint on this warrior?

The warriors have many different expressions. Some are smiling and look happy, but others are frowning and look stern. Each figure is **unique**.

How do you think this warrior is feeling?

Fields of Figures

Field for the British Isles is a sculpture by Antony Gormley. Like the Terracotta Army, it is made up of thousands of clay sculptures.

However, these clay figures are much simpler and smaller than the terracotta soldiers, and they haven't been painted.

Antony Gormley asked school children and their families to make the clay figures. The figures had to be hand-sized with deep eyes, but those were the only rules.

They were made over a week, dried in the sun and then baked in a kiln. Finally, the figures were arranged on the floor facing forwards. The figures aren't painted, but you can still see different shades of colour when you look at them together.

There are about 40 000 clay figures in this photograph. They completely fill the space they are in.

They didn't use a mould to make the figures – each one is hand-crafted.

From a distance, they all look very similar, but if you look closely you can see that each one is unique. Which is your favourite?

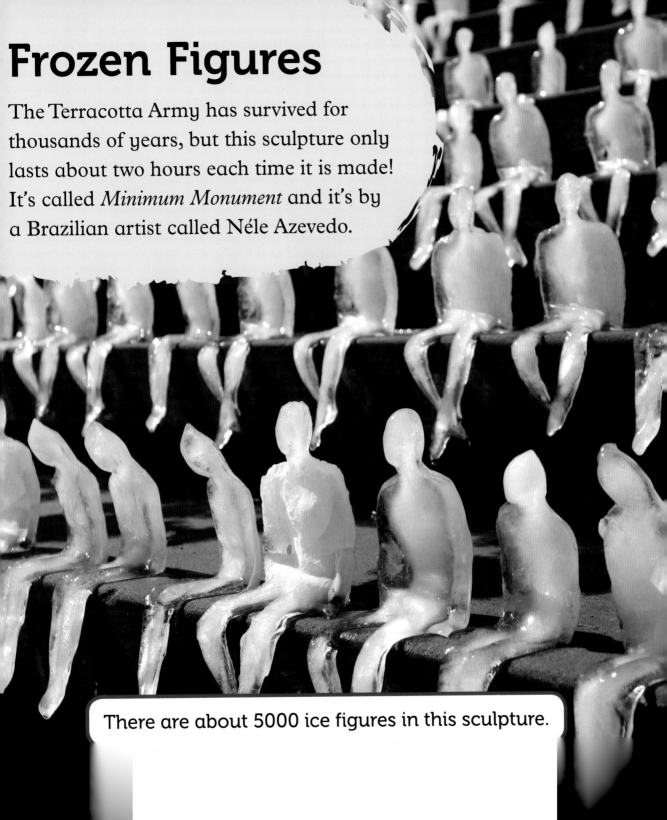

Frozen Figures

The Terracotta Army has survived for thousands of years, but this sculpture only lasts about two hours each time it is made! It's called *Minimum Monument* and it's by a Brazilian artist called Néle Azevedo.

There are about 5000 ice figures in this sculpture.

It's made by freezing water in moulds made from plastic bottles. Then the ice is scraped into shape and the figures are frozen again. Finally, the frozen figures are arranged on steps in public places like town squares.

The ice melts quickly so volunteers help the artist to arrange them. Then the figures are left to melt in the sunshine.

Minimum Monument makes some people remember friends and family. It makes others think about protecting the environment.

What does it make you think about?

Giant Heads

Easter Island is a remote island in the Pacific Ocean. It is the home of nearly 900 sculptures of people. Unlike *Minimum Monument*, these sculptures are enormous! On average, they are about 4 metres tall – that's over twice as tall as a real person.

These huge sculptures are called moai (*say* moa-igh).

The first sculptures were made about 800 years ago and more were sculpted over the next 500 years. Most of them are arranged with their backs to the sea, looking towards the people who live on the island.

They were sculpted out of huge stones on the island. Some have hair made of a red coloured stone.

When they were first made, they had eyes made of coral and a special black stone that was polished to make it shine.

Some experts believe that they were sculptures of real people who lived on the island.

Many of the sculptures have beautiful **engravings** on their backs.

In this picture, we can only see the head of the sculpture. The rest of the body is buried underground.

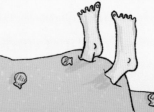

An Underwater Village

If you go snorkelling or scuba-diving in the sea near Cancún in Mexico, you'll see more than fish in the water. In fact, you'll be visiting the Underwater Museum of Art.

A group of sculptors have been creating concrete sculptures and sinking them on to the sea bed.

One of the biggest sculptures in the museum is called *The Silent Evolution* by Jason deCaires Taylor. He made concrete figures of over 400 people from a nearby village, including children, parents, elderly people and fishermen. Then he lowered the concrete figures on to the sea floor.

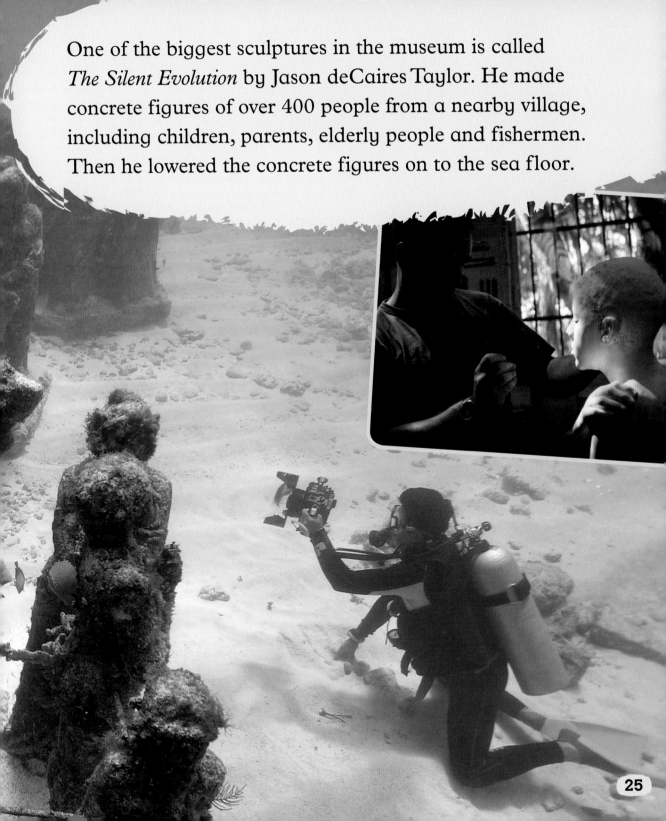

The artist made some parts of the figures rough and left other parts smooth. Coral, seaweed and other plants and animals started to grow on these rough parts. They look like hair and clothes.

The sculpture has become an amazing new home for sea life.

Tourists used to dive around a natural coral **reef** nearby, and the reef was becoming damaged.

Now, tourists visit the underwater museum instead, so the natural reef is protected from harm.

This sculpture is called *The Dream Collector*.

What do you think is inside the bottles?

Endless Possibilities

Every sculpture in this book is of a group of people, but they are all very different.

Sculptures can be tiny or enormous. They can be moulded from all sorts of materials, such as clay or ice. They can last for thousands of years or only minutes.

Why not make your very own sculpture of a group of people? What would it look like? How many figures would you make? What would you use to make it? Would it be big or small?

It's up to you – you're the sculptor!

Glossary

engravings: pictures or symbols carved on materials like wood or stone

figures: people-shaped objects

hollow: empty inside

kiln: an oven for baking clay

lacquer: a liquid used to decorate wood and pottery

moulds: containers used to shape soft material or liquid

reef: a line of rocks or coral near the surface of the sea

sculptor: an artist who makes sculptures

sculptures: works of art made by carving or shaping materials like clay, stone and ice

solid: something that has no space inside it

terracotta: reddish-brown clay that has been baked

unique: the only one of its kind, unlike anything else

warrior: someone who is in an army

Index

Look Back, Explorers

When was the first warrior in the Terracotta Army discovered?

How many ice figures are in the sculpture *Minimum Monument*?

What is one similarity between the Terracotta Army and *Field for the British Isles*?

What questions would you ask the artist who made *The Silent Evolution*?

The moai sculptures were *arranged* with their backs to the sea. What other words mean the same as *arranged*?

Did you find out where this sculpture is?

What's Next, Explorers?

Now you know about sculptures from all over the world, go on a magic key adventure with Biff and Anneena to China ...

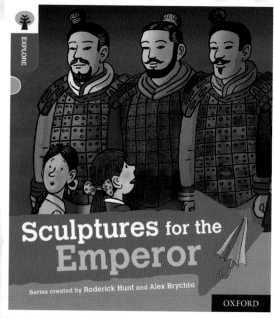

Sculptures for the Emperor

Series created by Roderick Hunt and Alex Brychta

OXFORD

Explorer Challenge
for *Sculptures for the Emperor*

Find out who has this moustache ...